Published by Nauset Press
nausetpress.com

NAUSET
PRESS

New York

ISBN 978-0692676936

Design by Nauset Press

The Land & Her Vanity

A SINGULAR PROSE POEM

Wyoming, U.S.A.

BY ROBERTA HARPER-MCINTOSH

We live where you look across

to the horizon and you see:

4

space . . . s p a c e

To move, breathe, think, and not be seen.

You figure other people are optional.

You don't see evidence of other people

once your vision has shot past the

last few houses in a sloping development.

You see what looks like nothing:

yellowed grasses

that make brown with the dirt;

rises and bends in the land,

and maybe

a shadow or two...

...and then sky.

It calls to you to cross it and

see the next stretch,

just like it, or not.

And, unless you wanted something from it,

something you couldn't see but you knew was there,

like gold or water

or you knew there was something else after that,

like life after death – say, mountains –

you would not want to cross it

any more than you would

want to cross the moon,

which is nothing but the moon,

and always white and never changing.

That's if you don't know this land.

If you know it a little better,

you've seen it at different times of day,

when the light strikes it altogether differently

and you've seen how it changes colors:

White waves in the morning...

...flat brown with grass at noon,

with the purple growing under it in the afternoon

until the evening takes over

and bleeds up into the tips of the grass

as the cold settles down into its roots,

and the blues and greens of sage come to life,

the pink of the earth and the purple of the sky

showing their secret love affair that noon hides.

And then there's the gentle light of early morning,

with mist, maybe, the dips and rises not yet awake,

still lazy and dallying and closer-seeming than

the gritty eye of the prospector will ever know.

You could walk into the hills

in the dewy morning

and hear them whisper about each other

to you, if you knew how to listen.

You would see the flickers of the birds—

swallows, finches, mourning doves—

darting and delighting in the gentle garden,

where you still see little flowers

that you haven't yet named,

you see the tiny seeds, like little pillboxes,

that they gather,

and hear their thoughtful coos and trills,

enveloped in the damp for now.

Then, once you know the garden and its wiles,

once you have rested in her

and let out your breath

and given up your ideas

and been still so you can see,

even at noon you see

that the grass is the prairie's skin,

that it stretches fully furred up over every rise

and across the belly and sides and haunches

of the land as it naps and watches

and huffs and waits and sleeps,

depending on the light and the season

and the sky and the air.

You see too where the land

has been shaved bald by overgrazing;

you know where cattle have been and been again,

nuzzling the irritable skin for that last blade of green,

and sauntered on,

not finding much here, planting their hooves

into every inch of the soil in a season,

but reaping no harvest.

You see the tired dryness of those hills,

how they're mostly dirt and

have no face to turn to you as the sun

and clouds move across the sky.

A few years of this and you see a

shame-faced nakedness that has turned away

and gone within, leaving its dried-up skin to greet you

while it withdraws from the sky

and the birds

and the wind

and won't peek out for the long stretch.

You'll look but you won't see,

the way a shaved cat

would never show its face.

But if you're a lover, you'll see the land

though she hides

and turns away from you.

You'll see the way her skin drinks the rain,

if the rain is gentle enough,

and the way the light still caresses her

even though she's gone within

to indefinite and stubborn hibernation.

You know about the birds and their twitters

and her morning preening and whispering,

the sheen of her grassy fur and

the long stretches of her generosity

when she's purring and awake,

and how she sleeps in the day's glare

and how you must visit

her when the moon caresses her...

...and the clouds have brought her her drink

and she has coaxed the flowers and birds

out of hiding

and the lizards only

      watch and wait

           for their rocks to burn again.

Then you can watch as she lounges and

dreams and plays in her lazy way.

You stand there, among the rusts and purples

and pinks and sages that

the drivers in shimmering trucks

snaking across her

will never see.

You might swirl in your cup a little tea, made

straight from the tiny yellow bulbs that

grow on her wounds and give away her apple-scented

charm, and watch for her, and wait for some

seeds to pop and take root and begin to replace

her lost full and glossy coat.

If you have a footing here

and have taken rocks in hand,

you'll say yes or no to cattle this year;

but if not,

if you're a wanderer and watcher

like the antelope that nestle in

her soft spots,

you'll hope for the best

and coax her colors out

when the rain kisses her,

and go and sit inside

or drive off for weeks at a time,

to return when she's in a better mood, for a bit,

to sit and swirl your tea

and watch the stars with her

and tell her stories of them

to lift her gloom.

www.ingramcontent.com/pod-product-compliance
Lightning Source LLC
LaVergne TN
LVHW010032070426
835508LV00005B/303